Creating the New American
TOWN HOUSE

First published in the
United States of America in 2005 by
RIZZOLI INTERNATIONAL PUBLICATIONS, INC.
300 Park Avenue South
New York, NY 10010
www.rizzoliusa.com

ISBN: 0-8478-2712-7
LCCN: 2005901270

Photography credits: page 240

Design by Dung Ngo / www.NGOstudio.com

Printed and bound in China
2005 2006 2007 2008 2009 / 10 9 8 7 6 5 4 3 2 1

Creating the New American

TOWN HOUSE

Alexander Gorlin

TABLE OF CONTENTS

The houses be of fair and gorgeous building, and on the street side they stand joined together in a long row through the whole street without any partition or separation.

—Thomas More, *Utopia*

Since my first book on the town house (*New American Town House*, Rizzoli: 2000), this building type has begun to fulfill its promise as a tool in the reconstruction of the inner city. Both as an infill and as a house type to rebuild entire neighborhoods, the town house, with its comfortable, human scale, has been in the vanguard of the return of the suburbanites to the city. Aging baby boomers have become dissatisfied with suburbia and its frequently vacuous sprawl, its lack of vitality, and have realized that the critical density of urban living, with its walk-able and pedestrian scale, is essential to their full enjoyment of life. With children grown, empty nesters, as well as younger people, are returning to the vibrancy of the city, to live in town houses of all sizes and economic incarnations. This book documents the trend by presenting the best examples of town houses built in the last few years in the United States.

In recent years, in building, there has been an emphasis on the individual town house as opposed to the block-long rows that once made up American cities such as Baltimore, New York, and Boston. Of course, good urban examples of row houses can be found still in San Francisco, San Diego, and, soon, in the Nehemiah town houses in Brooklyn, and elsewhere. Presently, among world cities, Amsterdam has been among the most ambitious in this regard; Eastern Docklands, a vast area of the city, was built entirely with modern town houses as the module of reconstruction.

By definition the town house is a house in town, the city. Traditionally, this building type derives its structure from two parallel walls, which ultimately dictate the form with which we are familiar; frequently, it is one of a group, joined by common sidewalls. It is an extremely old form of urban dwelling, as evidenced in numerous sources—from the facades discovered on over-3,500-year-old faience plaques from ancient Crete, to the ubiquitous Roman and Greek town houses described in the first century B.C.E. by Roman architectural theorist Vitruvius.

Pompeii and Herculaneum are cities almost entirely built out of these parallel wall urban houses. The town house is unique as both a structural and spatial building type in that the walls that hold up the house also establish a strong modular sensibility that can be replicated to define the streets and plazas of the traditional and contemporary city. Efficient and economical to build, when repeated in series, the cost is lowered as a result of a shared party wall structure. As opposed to the freestanding suburban house, the town or row house implies its neighbor; it is the urban house par excellence. In Thomas More's *Utopia*, the ideal city of Amaurote is composed of town houses: "The houses be of fair and gorgeous building, and on the street side they stand joined together in a long row through the whole street without any partition or separation. The streets be twenty foot broad. On the back side of the houses, through the whole length of the street, lie gardens enclosed round about with the back side of the streets."

The town house is both an individual unit capable of personal expression and, as well, the embodiment of an urban capacity to shape the public space of the city. In Florence, town houses shaped the Piazza del Duomo to compliment the mass of the Duomo; in Bath, they curve into crescent and horseshoe shaped plazas. From the Place Vendome and the Place de Vosges in Paris to the squares of London and Washington Square Park in New York, town houses shape the outdoor rooms of the city.

From city to city, variations in the town house reflect the values and priorities of the particular culture and region of which each city is a part. Different circumstances help determine both the plan and appearance of the facade. In Venice, town houses are wide along the canal and not too deep; whereas in Amsterdam, the canal frontage is narrow but the property often reaches back to the next canal at the rear garden. In Italy, *bella figura*, a public face is very important, so a wider facade is desirable. In Amsterdam and London, however, a more practical emphasis on real estate value is apparent in the crowding of more town houses on each block, resulting in narrow facades; this became the model for the American city—from New York, the former New Amsterdam, to Boston, Baltimore, and Philadelphia.

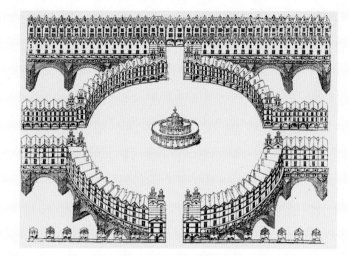

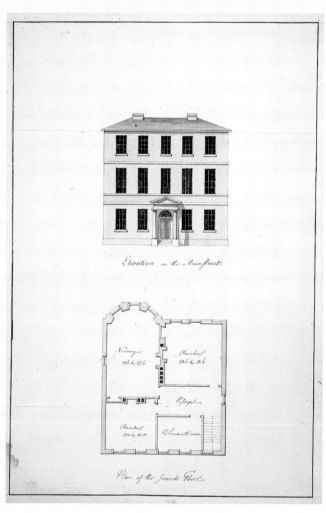

From the days of Vitruvius in the first century B.C.E. to Alberti in the Renaissance to today, there has always been a dialogue, a push and pull relationship in our notions of the city and the country house. Written in Book Five of his **The Ten Books of Architecture** over five hundred years ago, architect and theorist Leone Battista Alberti's description of this dialogue remains valid today:

The Country House and Town House for the Rich differ in this Circumstance; that they use their Country House chiefly for a Habitation in the Summer, and their Town House as a convenient Place of Shelter in the Winter. In their Country House therefore they enjoy the Pleasures of Light, Air, Spacious Walks and fine Prospects; in Town, there are but few Pleasures, but those of Luxury and the Night. It is sufficient therefore if in Town they can have an Abode that does not want any Conveniences for living with Health, Dignity and Politeness: But yet, as far as the Want of Room and Prospect will admit, our Habitation in Town should not be without any of the Delicacies of that in the Country. We should be sure to have a good Courtyard, Portico, Places for Exercise, and some Garden.

If you are cramped for Room, and cannot make all your Conveniences upon one Floor, make several Stories, by which means you may make the Members of your House as large as is necessary; and if the Nature of your foundation will allow it, dig Places under Ground for your Wines, Oil, Wood, and even some Part of your Family, and such a Basement will add Majesty to your whole Structure. Thus you may build as many Stories as you please, till you have fully provided for all the Occasions of your Family.

Storage has always been a problem, even in simpler times, Alberti continues:

No Store-rooms should be wanting for laying up Corn, Fruits, and all Manner of Tools, Implements and Household-stuff; nor Places for divine Worship; nor Wardrobes for the

Women. Nor must you be without convenient Store-rooms for laying up Cloths designed for your Family to wear only on Holidays, and Arms both defensive and offensive, Implements for all Sorts of Works in Wool, Preparations for the Entertainment of Guests and all Manner if of Necessities for any extraordinary Occasions.

Until the beginning of the modern period of architecture in the early part of the twentieth century, the town house remained fairly constant. Especially in plan, the town house was restricted in the organization of its rooms due to masonry construction. This kind of structure is basically inflexible regarding the internal placement of walls, which must be similar from floor to floor. However, even with similar construction, there is great variation between the glassy and open facades of the old Amsterdam town house and the lugubriously dark brownstones of nineteenth-century New York.

Modern architecture, with its steel and reinforced concrete construction, opened up new spatial configurations within the town house. Rooms could now be radically shifted around each level, as explored by architects such as Le Corbusier, Pierre Chareau, and Reitveldt; culminating in the dazzling exploded space of Paul Rudolph's own house in New York.

In Le Corbusier's Maison Cook, the intricate circulation of stairs and ramps intertwine with internal volumes, of single and double height. The roof is utilized as a garden, so that all horizontal areas are habitable, one of his "Five Points of the New Architecture." Spatially, of Le Corbusier's four types, the town house represented the prism (a rectangular volume), the "most difficult" in that one must design within a restrictive space, a form that is perfect on the exterior, hiding the labyrinthine circulation and volumetric play of the interior.

The Schroeder-Schraeder House by Gerrit Rietveldt of 1922, one of the seminal modern houses of the twentieth century, is in fact a town house, although it is never analyzed in that context. The end row house on a block in Utrecht, its facade is composed of a series of floating planes of De Stijl color—red,

blue, and yellow, against a background of white, gray, and black. As opposed to the solid corner of classical tradition, the exterior planes never meet and open to the space of the flat Dutch landscape. The interior, with its complex, interlocking, puzzle-like space, remains for subsequent town houses the ne plus ultra touchstone of modernism. The interior walls all slide apart to allow for maximum flexibility in what is actually quite a small space. For all its innovation, Reitveldt maintains the rhythm of the adjoining town houses, but interpreted and transformed into a modern idiom.

Another powerful precedent for the modern town house was Mies van der Rohe's modern interpretation of classicism: Vitruvius's orders of architecture distilled into elegant armatures of bronze and steel. Mies's early town houses at the Weissenhof Housing Exhibition in Stuttgart, 1927, was a block of apartments of the Siedlungen type, in the International Style of horizontal window bands, punctuated by stair towers. Later, having moved to the United States from Germany, his moderate income town houses of Lafayette Park in Detroit are essentially modules of the structural frame concept that motivated his large office and apartment towers. Set within a lush green landscape, each house has large panes of glass that suggest a grand scale and elegance. When Mies applied these same modules to giant towers, the same unit, relative to many others, often took on an anonymous and alienating character.

A final example of a modern town house that remains an inspiration for the contemporary American manifestation is Pierre Chareau's masterpiece, the Maison de Verre (The Glass House) in Paris of 1929. This Parisian hotel de ville is veiled by a mysterious translucent facade of square glass block with a circular imprint, which allows a milky light to illuminate the interior space. Designed originally for Pierre Dalsace, a gynecologist, it is both his home and office. It perfectly represents that quandary of early modern architecture's fascination with the efficiency of the machine as a model for life and its corresponding lack of comfort. The Maison de Verre was one of the few to bridge that gap by extracting the sensuous possibili-

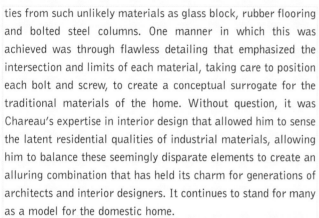

Right: Philip Johnson, The Rockefeller Town House, New York, NY
Bottom right: Robert A.M. Stern, Park Avenue Town House, New York, New York, 1975

Opposite: Shelton Mindel Associates, Historic Town House, New York, NY 2004

ties from such unlikely materials as glass block, rubber flooring and bolted steel columns. One manner in which this was achieved was through flawless detailing that emphasized the intersection and limits of each material, taking care to position each bolt and screw, to create a conceptual surrogate for the traditional materials of the home. Without question, it was Chareau's expertise in interior design that allowed him to sense the latent residential qualities of industrial materials, allowing him to balance these seemingly disparate elements to create an alluring combination that has held its charm for generations of architects and interior designers. It continues to stand for many as a model for the domestic home.

What is modern about the town houses represented in this book? How modernism can be defined within the context of a spatial type that has remained constant for thousands of years is a question with many answers. As the space of a painting is constrained by the edges of its canvas, a town house is constrained by its frame—the parallel walls that encompass the space within. And, like modern painting, which exploded previously held conceptions of what art could be, vastly expanding what was possible, the modern town house is much freer than its predecessors to explore themes, ideas, and concepts, enlarging our very conception of this important urban form. In these modern houses, materials are explored for their own characteristics, with an emphasis on the "raw" as opposed to the Straussian "cooked." Wood is wood, metal is metal. Demonstrated here is a kind of material fundamentalism that expresses a joy in the revelation of the making of the forms. In the interpenetration of spaces, the intricate labyrinth of staircases, or the dramatic use of materials and light, a sense of excitement percolates through these houses.

ADVICE FROM THE ARCHITECT

Suppose you are building or renovating a town house—what are the things to look for—or pitfalls to avoid? Having designed and built town houses across America, I will try to share my experience.

If you have fallen in love with the idea of living in a town house but cannot find one that fits your needs or just wish to embark on the adventure of designing and building your own dream house, then a road map is in order. The first decision is whether to build from scratch or to renovate. In many central cities there are existing town houses that are available but need major renovation, both in terms of program and structure. Either they were built in the nineteenth or early twentieth century and were designed with outdated kitchens and baths, or were renovated badly in the 1960s through the 1980s. Those of historical interest can be restored to their original details, while being updated with modern conveniences and appliances. Another more exciting direction is to view the entire ensemble as a shell with new construction to combine the best of the old and the new.

After finding a possible property through the internet, broker, or simply walking around the neighborhood you desire, a consulting engineer should check the property for problems with the structural, mechanical, and electrical systems. Subsequently, should you conclude that major construction is required, it is imperative that you check the local Building and Zoning Codes. There is no point in attempting to build something that is prohibited by the local municipality. There are numerous rules governing limitations in zoning, height limits, setbacks, build-able area, and landmark restrictions that are often very different not only from city to city but within specific zoning districts. This is the least glamorous, but most important part of the process.

A professional architect or code consultant can analyze these zoning and building codes that govern the size and placement of the town house. Often a real estate lawyer will need to be involved to navigate the rules and regulations. Sometimes a variance will be needed and then there is no guarantee that it

will be granted! Never take a lot at face value and certainly be wary of real estate brokers who promise that you too can build a similarly sized addition to the rear or on top of a town house, because your neighbors have done the same thing. Remember, the rules of municipal building departments change all the time. For example, in Chicago, rules regarding town houses go back to the great fire of 1886, which resulted in a required gap between each house. Attached town houses were therefore discouraged, even 120 years after the disaster! As has often been said, the law has little to do with reality and there is no better example than rules related to construction.

Hiring an architect can be a daunting task, but ask friends, read books and magazines, surf the internet, until someone catches your eye. Then call directly, and ask for the principal. Don't be shy, as most architects will take a call for a potential job. Explain your project briefly with size and a realistic budget in mind and ask for an interview—apart from talent, personal chemistry is essential, since you will spend probably two years with this architect and his or her firm to achieve your goals for a beautiful and comfortable home.

Left: Paul Rudolph, Hirsch/Halston Town House, New York. 1966
Below: Paul Rudolph, Hirsch/Halston Town House first floor plan

Opposite top: Rockwell Group, set for "Hairspray", 2002
Opposite bottom: Alexander Gorlin Architects, Chicago Town House, 2004

PLAN

The width and depth of lot are very important. In New York there are legendary narrow lots that are 12 to 14 feet wide; in this case, the house becomes one room wide, limiting how the internal space can be utilized. A width of 20 or 25 feet is ideal, allowing for two rooms side by side in width for bedrooms of decent size on either front or rear. The lot size is different from the space inside, since the sidewalls have a significant width, usually of at least 10 to 12 inches, that must be subtracted from the overall width of the town house.

AREA

This is initially a function of building codes and height restrictions, often based on a formula called FAR, the floor-area ratio. This is a zoning code that determines how much square footage can be built on a city lot; it is presented in multiples of the lot area itself, so that a FAR of 3 is three times the lot area. Since a town house is by definition built-up to the lot line left and right, the FAR is crucial especially if there is a height restriction as well. Traditionally, this is the reason many town houses in London and New York had one-half level below grade, to qualify as a basement, which is not considered in calculating FAR.

HEIGHT

Heights of floors should be related to the specific level of habitation; the main floor or piano nobile is historically either one-half floor or one floor above grade. This level should be at least 10 to 12 feet in height, although the width of the town house and therefore the proportion of the rooms must be taken into account. Rooms that are too tall for their width can feel awkward. The lower level can be 8 feet high, or even a bit less. Le Corbusier used the standard of 7 feet 6 inches (the height of a six-foot man reaching upwards) as his minimum height, but with people apparently growing taller with each generation, this may be too low. Upper floors can be 8 feet 6 inches or 9 feet high. If the house is custom designed, why not use Frank Lloyd Wright's device of relating the dimension of the room to the

client's height, perhaps to a dado or door height. In new construction, the public rooms can be double height or more—taking advantage of the structural possibilities of steel or concrete. Paul Rudolph's own town house must have at least 30 different levels and mezzanines within the upper two-and-one-half floors of his town house. "Don't assume anything" may be a good motto for a renovation in an old town house that could be 100 years old or more. Adding height to a basement might start out innocently, but will not always end that way. If the house is in a low lying area, it could be above a long buried spring; or, once you start digging, you may strike oil, and not in the way the Beverly Hillbillies did—rather, the source of your strike may be a neighbor's leaking oil tank.

ORGANIZATION AND ROOM TYPES

In planning your town house with your architect, make a program or list of rooms and spaces that you need, with approximate square footages and their adjacency requirements. This "wish list" will force you to think about how you live now and how you wish to live in the town house. The architect will also confront this list with the reality of your site and budget. Together, a creative synthesis is achieved that brings the project into fruition.

There is an inherent tension between the desire to have rooms open directly to the garden and those on the elevated piano nobile. Functionally and for circulation flow, the kitchen should open up to the dining room, breakfast area, and often to an informal "family" room. If the family room opens onto the garden, then the living room should be placed upstairs. Another possible organization is to have the kitchen, dining, and living rooms on the floor above the garden. The kitchen can open onto a deck that leads to the garden, which is a very pleasant arrangement. As in Pompeii, the town house garden is an extension of the interior rooms, and can be planted or paved to emphasize this relationship. Of course, care must be taken to avoid a deck that is too deep, which would make the rooms below too dark and dank. The orientation of the garden facade is paramount since, if it faces south, then the deck can create welcome shade, unless it faces a chilly northern exposure. If this is the case, then either eliminate the deck altogether or make it out of wood with slight gaps between the planks for a dappled light.

Kitchens in modern town houses are subject to the same considerations as in any home—they must allow for a functional organization, lots of light, built-in appliances, an island with bar stools for breakfast, cabinets that are conveniently located, and plenty of storage. One should decide if the kitchen should be visible or not, in a loft setting or in a separate room of its own. Historically, the kitchen was placed in the basement or ground floor level for convenience of delivery and access to the street for refuse removal. These considerations have not changed over time and there is much to be said for leaving the kitchen at grade level, opening onto the garden in the rear. If the kitchen is moved to the main level either one or one-half flight up, then one needs to carry groceries up and subsequently bring the garbage and recycling down stairs to the street.

Bedrooms are best placed upstairs to separate them from the more public spaces of the house. The master bedroom is usually placed above the main level and the children or guestrooms on the top floor. Bedrooms are located either on the street or garden side depending upon one's sensitivity to noise.

Another possibility is the master bedroom on the ground level with direct access to the garden; this could also be used for aging parents who visit, so that they don't need to climb a flight of stairs. On the other hand, one may place guestrooms far above to avoid having guests stay too long!

This leads to the issue of whether an elevator is necessary. It is often of interest especially thinking of the future when stairs are no longer the "stair master" of the gymnasium, but a necessary evil to be conquered on a daily basis. The problem is, an elevator takes up a lot of room, is expensive, and does not substitute for a stair but is, rather, supplemental. Also, there is the slight danger of being trapped in a broken elevator alone in the house. The elevator is definitely something to consider, but one must explore and analyze the positive and negative impact on the plan.

Because of the restricted space, bathrooms in town houses tend to be small. The standard size is 5-by-8 feet, compressing all the typical functions into one small room. At the beginning of the twentieth century this was an achievement of efficiency; in the twenty-first century, it shows a lack of imagination. When possible, separate the functions of the bathroom into three areas or zones: bathing, washing, and toilet area. The ultimate example of luxury is the Roman bath, with its great public baths for hot (caldarium), cold (frigidarium), and lukewarm water (tepidarium). Miniaturizing the nature of the Roman bath into a relatively tiny space requires creativity, but there are numerous examples in this book. Assigning each function its own space gives a much grander feeling to the bath. However, beware of allowing too much space for the bathroom, or you will be creating a poorly proportioned, McTown House, which must be avoided.

The family room and living room are really two different types of spaces—one for informal family events, the other for more formal gatherings. If there is a space problem, both can be used for either function. Usually, when the two rooms are joined, a more informal setting is implied, because it is difficult to transform an informal room into a formal one. In this case often photographs lie, and the rooms are cleaned up for their portrait.

STRUCTURE

The structure of the town house lies between and includes the parallel walls that define the property line. Beams support the floors that span from wall to wall, with internal non-supporting walls organized for specific rooms and places of activity. This allows for the front and rear facades to be as open as desired. The generally dark aspect of the New York brownstone owes as much to the tonality of the stone used for the facades as to the vertically proportioned windows, which were a matter of style, not structural limitation. Such windows make more sense for a Mediterranean town house, where it is sometimes desirable to keep out the harsh sun with shutters. The rise of modern architecture allowed a return to openness for the town house facade, which frequently employs large sheets of glass or glass block, that open up the interior to the light for a direct or translucent effect.

The structure of a town house disguises the fact that, unless the group was built all at once, the vertical walls are individually supported like soldiers in a row. During construction, care must be taken to assure that the new foundations do not undermine the neighboring structure.

If one chooses, it is possible to connect two floors with a double-height space of varying depth in order to allow for a very exciting spatial effect. Of course, double-height spaces within the confines of a town house are a great luxury; giving up space for architectural drama is the ultimate sacrifice in a town house. I remember, in the design of a town house in Seaside, my clients admired a house I had designed for myself, "Stairway to Heaven," in which a double-height living room opens onto the park of Ruskin Place. Within the same-size footprint they asked for a similar space, but then proceeded to list a series of rooms, which immediately filled in the double-height space. Unfortunately, you can't have it all. One learns quickly that all things are not possible in a town house, a microcosm of architecture and planning. The simple volume of rectangular space exemplified by the town house may be the most difficult to plan, but, when done well, it rewards one with great satisfaction.

Opposite: Alexander Gorlin Architect, Aqua Development Town Houses, Miami, Florida. 2005

Right: Alexander Gorlin Architects, New York Town House, 2002
Bottom: Alexander Gorlin Architects, New York Town House, construction drawing of stair

The walls of the town house are another element that can be considered in both a conceptual and functional manner. Although they are foremost structural, either the walls or the space between can animate the design. In the latter, the walls are considered secondary, and every effort is to be taken to minimize their depth so that the maximum space between the walls is opened for light and breadth. Where this is the concept, all services—plumbing, stairs, and circulation elements— should be concentrated and pressed to the sidewalls of the house. Everything is secondary to the space between the walls.

If the walls are considered dominant, then one can think of the walls as poche (pocket), or conceptual thickness, that can be thickened with services, closets, shelves even widened to fit the width of the stairs that run alongside the walls. This is most useful in a wide town house of 25 feet, where one can afford at least one wall of closets of two-foot depth without sacrificing the open quality of the facade. This kind of plan is one of nooks and crannies, an undulating surface like Renaissance church plans, where solid walls were carved and cut in order to accommodate different needs. At the same time a sense of depth and thickness is given to the walls that define the rooms. A famous example of poche, was Michelangelo's plan for St. Peters, which was so heavily carved up into niches and recesses that the Pope rejected it, since there were too many spaces for "nuns to be ravished."

CIRCULATION

Stairs are the heart of the town house—going up and down stairs defines the vertical nature of town house living as opposed to the "flat" or horizontality of the apartment. The concept of verticality in Bachelard's *The Poetics of Space* is the *axis mundi*, linking heaven and hell, the basement of horror films to the attic and the heaven of the roof garden. Stairs are either to follow the lines of the party walls and run alongside in an ascending plan or can double back at the center. When they are on the side they take up the least amount of room, but you need the proper length of town house or the arrangement will not work. The central stair can be hidden or exposed, and can be a theatrical statement as in Duchamp's *Nude Descending a Staircase*, and can extend easily to the roof. There are many variations that use both types of circulation, such as in Le Corbusier or Adolf Loos plans. In Dutch and Palladian houses, stairs are hidden; whereas in French town houses the stairs are prominent—the idea of the public promenade versus private coming and going is explicit.

Finally, the culmination of the vertical path can be the roof terrace atop the town house. To most fully utilize the land displaced on the ground plane, a roof garden is the most charming and potentially fantastic space. This cosmic complement to the windowless basement is open to the sky. Here, a small living area or office with a bar or barbecue is possible, as well. Or, as in "Stairway to Heaven" in Seaside, a spiral stair can reach up into the space of a modern widow's walk from which to view the horizon. Examples of inspiring possibilities abound. A second town house at Seaside has a hot tub on the roof of the terrace living area, a private Shangri-la open to a magnificent view. It has become clear that in these houses quite a lot can be achieved within the confines of a relatively small area. The town house is a puzzle of space that, with imagination, can be solved in ever more rewarding ways.

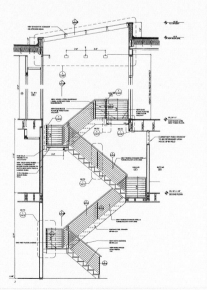

CHRISTIAN HUBERT
STUDIO

DAVID SALLE TOWN HOUSE
BROOKLYN, NEW YORK

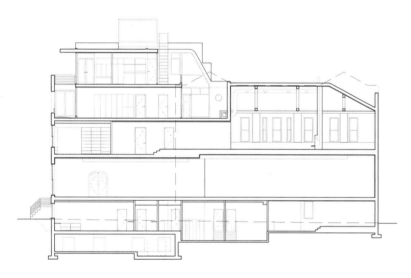

This town house for the painter David Salle combines two structures, one a former Masonic Temple and the other a dilapidated house on a Brooklyn corner. In order to unify the composition, a curving roof canopy of zinc drapes between the two buildings, housing a new three-story extension. Under this canopy is a series of roof terraces and balconies that afford both intimate areas of contemplation and distant views of the urban landscape. Retaining some of the secretive sensibility of its former use, the house presents a neutral exterior only to open up into beautifully detailed rooms with numerous finishes ranging from concrete to hand plastered walls and a luxurious series of exotic and domestic woods. The two formerly separate houses are treated quite differently inside—the older, more distinguished house has been restored to its former glory with intricate details, while the other was stripped and reconstructed in a modern idiom. A large painting studio dominates the main level, with the living spaces for the family on the upper three floors, connected by a dramatic stair. A gym, guestroom, and garage are located in the basement level. The culmination of the house is unquestionably the master bathroom, a surprisingly serene spa in downtown Brooklyn, a double height space opening onto its own private terrace off the master bath room. Like a geode, this house is packed full of sparkling treats once one enters the private realm of its interior. (David Fratianne, Associate Architect)

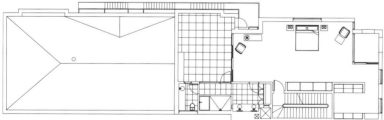

THIRD FLOOR PLAN

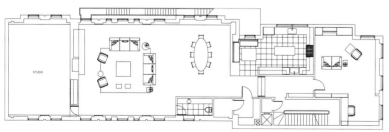

SECOND FLOOR PLAN

ROBERT M. GURNEY
ARCHITECT

CALVERT STREET TOWN HOUSE
WASHINGTON, D.C.

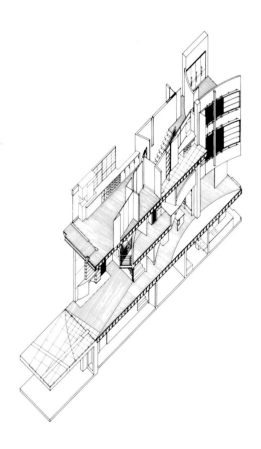

A 4,000-square-foot residence in the Kalorama-Adams Morgan area in Washington, this house was formerly a neighborhood eyesore, filled with debris and inhabited by vagrants and pigeons. This total renovation transforms the residence into a daring new modern town house inside an old shell. The most is made of the house's long, narrow footprint—17 feet wide at the front narrowing to 13 feet—by subverting the traditional orthogonal plan suggested by the site's limitations.

A curving geometry has been created, and is especially evident on the second and third stories. Thus, despite the home's narrow confines, curved lofted spaces open the second and third stories to views to the main floor. The elliptical curve, based on a ten-degree diagonal running from a rear corner of the house to a point near the center, results in a unique rearrangement of each floor. This varies the in-line, "railroad car" plan that such a narrow lot might otherwise dictate.

The living room is now open to natural light, not only from the lower level of the new window walled rear facade, but to light filtering down from the facade through the upper levels, which would otherwise have been blocked. The curved wall above is further enlivened by the use of rectangular concrete pillars and walls, sandblasted glass, translucent panels, maple, and steel. A warm combination of colors and textures admit and modulate the light and respond to the urban context.

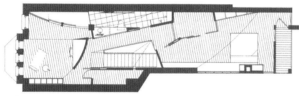

THIRD FLOOR PLAN

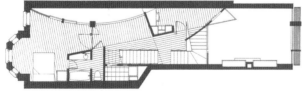

SECOND FLOOR PLAN

FIRST FLOOR PLAN

WESLEY WEI
ARCHITECTS

TOWN HOUSE WITH SIX WALLS
PHILADELPHIA, PENNSYLVANIA

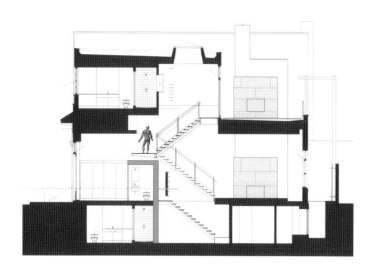

This renovation and addition to an 1895 commercial building in Philadelphia, originally a wholesale liquor store, creates a modern town house and workspace. It also houses the owners' (a painter/ bookmaker and an author) collection of art and artifacts from around the world. The 14-foot ceiling height and the double-wide town house lot give the space an open loft-like quality.

Described by the architect as a palimpsest, the residence is marked by new architectural elements deftly overlayed upon traces of original details. The original patina of the brick and cement party wall frame a new double-height steel and cedar stair. Markings on the wall are supplemented by notes and details from the building's original construction and a text painted by the owner. Other original elements are preserved within the modern design as reminders of the historical and spatial fabric of the property, including pressed tin ceilings and portions of the storefront. Continuing the theme of old and new, the master bath combines modern plumbing fittings and an old claw foot tub.

Six freestanding 15-inch-thick cedar walls demarcate the spaces. These walls also create a novel space for the display of sculptural pieces, artifacts such as stones and eggs, and even writings. Niches, portals and recesses, like the shadow boxes employed by the artist Joseph Cornell, reveal a variety of hidden treasures complimenting the palimpsest of architectural styles.

FIRST FLOOR PLAN

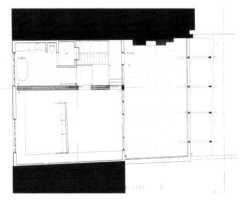

SECOND FLOOR PLAN

SHELTON, MINDEL & ASSOCIATES

HISTORIC TOWN HOUSE
NEW YORK, NEW YORK

FIRST FLOOR PLAN

"Archaeology, then architecture," so the architects describe this restoration of, and the addition of two stories to, a Greek Revival town house in Manhattan. To restore and further open the spacious rooms of the original structure, the top two floors of the residence were gutted. Excavation proceeded downward, resulting in an enlarged ground floor kitchen and the creation of a lower garden area. Minimal changes were made to the street facade, with the rooftop addition setback on both street and garden elevations to avoid variation from the historical character of the neighborhood.

The house culminates in the penthouse level, where a large skylight and a roof structure cantilevered toward the north incorporate views of communal gardens and the Manhattan skyline. The program incorporates terraces and a sitting room with office space. The new fourth floor is tied into the facade with an over-scaled bronze steel window, which also provides the family room with natural light and views to the garden. Minimally furnished with a Jean Prouvé table and lamp, this room appears to float in the treetops.

Second- and third-story bedrooms and sitting rooms are spacious and house a collection of important twentieth-century furniture, restored and reupholstered to blend harmoniously with furniture, rugs, and millwork custom designed by the architects, as well as with the painstakingly restored classical details.

The garden and terrace are paved with the same cinza limestone as the adjoining kitchen and sitting room. A sandblasted glass platform filters light into the basement. A light bronzed steel stair floats down to a patio area with a full-story wall of water that reflects light and fills a pool. Four trees and a dished circular puddle enliven the rear garden.

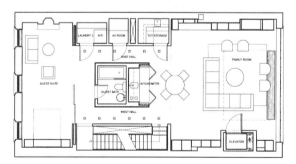

FOURTH FLOOR PLAN

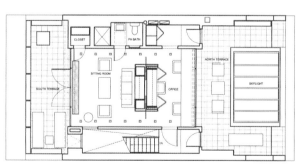

PENTHOUSE PLAN

MARPILLERO POLLAK
ARCHITECTS

DUANE STREET TOWN HOUSE
NEW YORK, NEW YORK

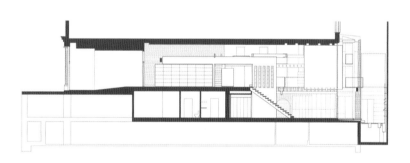

To reconfigure this nineteenth-century manufacturing facility into a contemporary town house, the architects began by removing a 12-foot-by-18-foot section of the first floor. This cut and the corresponding removal of another similarly sized section of the rear yard extension transformed the dark basement into a light-filled atrium, with a 26-foot-high window opening to the newly enlarged garden.

The basement, ground floor, and mezzanine levels each gracefully combine work and living spaces, with an office at the front facing the street. A hybrid construction of vertical circulation and book storage mediates between these spaces: the office stair-bookshelf extends from the basement to mezzanine, composed of wood and stone below and of a transparent metal grill above. The stair terminates in a balcony of the same material on the mezzanine, which houses a lofted bedroom and provides additional vantage points from which to admire the garden.

The garden itself is landscaped with luminescent white river-stone and vegetation. Uniquely angled mirrors are attached to an adjacent building, to reflect strips of sky, sun, and clouds. The basement is thus opened to the abstracted landscape of the garden intercut with views of the sky above.

The full height of the original west brick wall is continuously exposed and joined to the ceiling as a unified element, allowing light to penetrate the space fully. Original timber joists are displaced to wrap and frame the intervention, enclosing the intimate but open dining room behind the basement atrium. These joists also act as a handrail on the upper stairs and mezzanine, a bridge from the century-old walls to the modern interior.

STREET LEVEL FLOOR PLAN

GARDEN LEVEL FLOOR PLAN

1100 ARCHITECTS

VILLAGE TOWN HOUSE
NEW YORK, NEW YORK

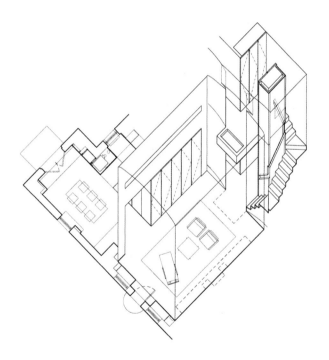

This deceptively simple, yet luxuriously decadent renovation of a town house in Manhattan is defined by its brilliantly light and airy feeling, emphasized and complemented by floors of dark maple. Originally a traditional pre-war town house, the plan remains relatively unchanged with a double height living room; with kitchen, dining, and bedrooms on the adjacent floors. Using a minimalist vocabulary with sharp lines and edges, walls and ceilings appear to float effortlessly on glowing clouds of light. These ribbons of light either amplify or dissolve the boundary between old and new, and flood each room with light from within and without.

The space is defined by openness and unity of form. Light fixtures and hardware are designed for minimum visibility. Walls appear paper-thin. Wall-to-floor cabinets traverse the living room and turn into the kitchen, joining the rooms seamlessly while maintaining the autonomy of each space. When closed, the cabinets blend unnoticeably into both rooms.

Soft blonde wood-toned chairs and chaise lounge give the double-height atrium/living room a feeling of *luxe, calme et volupte*. This centerpiece of the residence is minimally furnished and prismatically illuminated by the front window wall. Behind the room, a simple stair leads to the upstairs bedroom and bath. Even the handrail here is sunken into the wall for minimal intrusiveness. An apse-like space between the upstairs rooms looks down into the atrium.

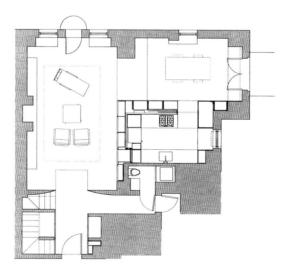

MAIN LEVEL FLOOR PLAN

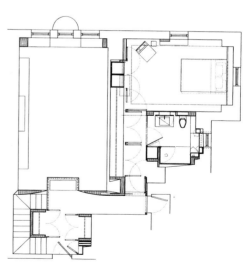

UPPER LEVEL FLOOR PLAN

VALERIO DEWALT
TRAIN ASSOCIATES

DOBLIN TOWN HOUSE
CHICAGO, ILLINOIS

This single story variation on the town house typology, used as a factory and commercial space throughout the twentieth century, maintains a strong industrial character in its twenty-first-century residential reincarnation. A structural steel frame and two giant galvanized steel "scissors doors" (24 feet wide by 12 feet high) define this single-story living space, supported by a grid of columns, 16 foot on center. Structural steel sections are suspended from surrounding masonry walls, and extend into the garden beyond the rear window wall, marked by a large steel truss. The rear yard and garden sit astride a hidden garage connected to the rear.

Either totally closed to the street or completely open, the mechanical steel doors open to reveal a space divided into three zones, with the living space sandwiched between two open garden areas. The secretive facade hides a spartanly furnished, yet spatially extravagant living area open to the vast, Midwest sky. A contrast of scale and materials is evident throughout the house, with giant diagonal trusses crossing one's line of sight and large expanses of glass, clear and translucent, seen against the long brick wall of the original factory building.

A bath/dressing room in one corner and a kitchen in the other anchor the living space. The kitchen and living room are illuminated and opened to the garden through the rear window wall. Even the bathroom, provided with privacy by translucent frosted glass, offers garden views and natural light through clear glass slats located around and above the shower.

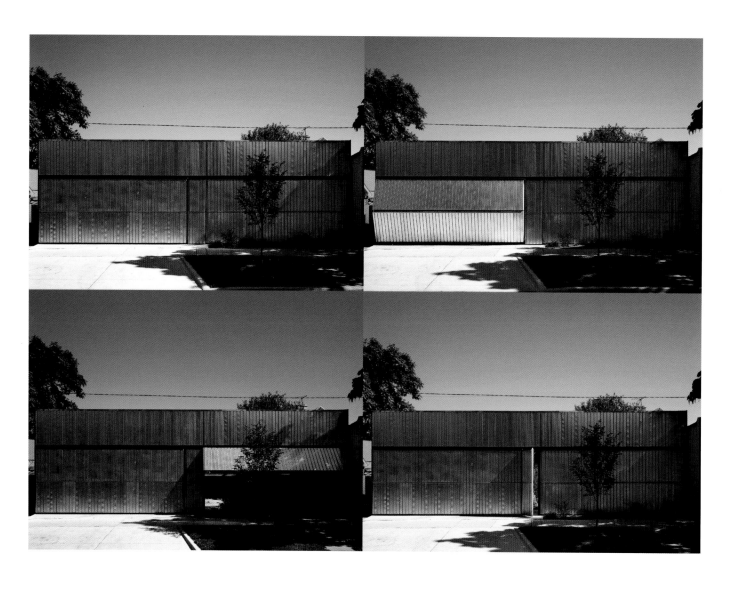

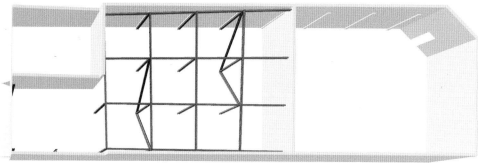

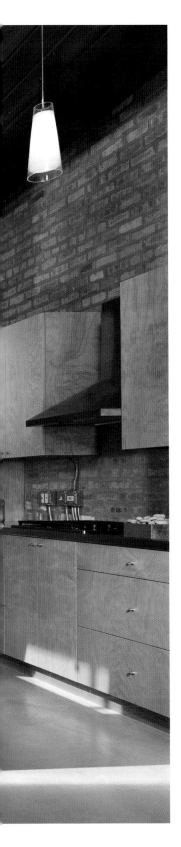

ALEXANDER GORLIN
ARCHITECTS

NEW YORK TOWN HOUSE
NEW YORK, NEW YORK

Set back 25 feet from the street, this black glass jewel of a town house has become a landmark that defines the neighborhood around it. Originally built in 1958, the shabby two-story structure had fallen into disrepair, and was completely redesigned, extended vertically, and in part restored. Mid-century modern was here brought into the twenty-first century. The new glass facade of the house announces its presence on the street, and a red door marks the entry once hidden inside the low brick wall defining the private precinct of the house. Inside, an open loft space of living, dining, and kitchen are open to the exterior with large glass walls on either side. A new staircase with open treads leads to the upper levels, within an atrium filled with light from the expansive skylight above. The second level has two children's bedrooms with a master bedroom on the street side. The master bath, with walls and floors of white statuary slab marble and glass, is

open to the bedroom with a long line of elegant pear wood closets leading from one space to the other. The addition of the third level is marked by glass block floors that allow light to penetrate deep into the floors below. The culmination of the house is the media room, which is acoustically isolated and open on one side to a terrace and on the other to the atrium with extremely clear low iron content glass. The room is framed by pear wood cabinets, which hold the owners extensive collection of CDs within a double layered system of shelves and doors. On this upper level there is, as well, a guest room, and an office. On the half level below the street is the playfully colored children's playroom and exercise area. A Zen-inspired stone and moss garden provides a contemplative vestibule or air lock to allow a transition from the hectic city street to the peaceful home within.

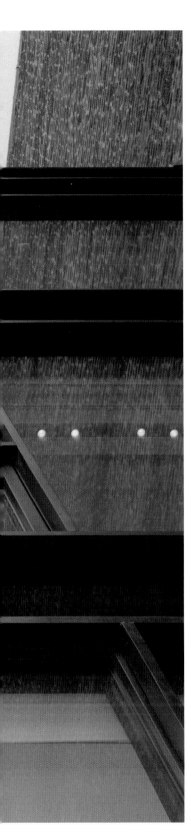

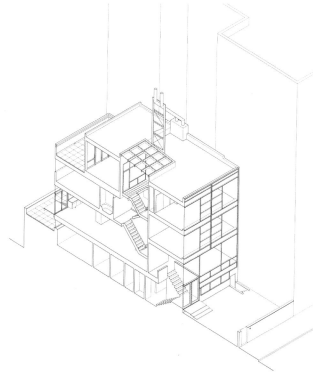

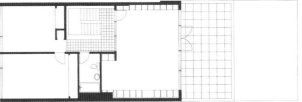

THIRD FLOOR PLAN

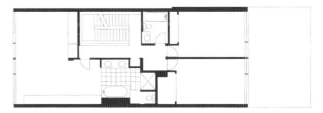

SECOND FLOOR PLAN

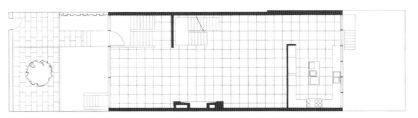

FIRST FLOOR PLAN

MACK ARCHITECTS

BAY CITY/ABBOTT KINNEY TOWN HOUSES
LOS ANGELES, CALIFORNIA

These three town houses take advantage of new zoning codes along the Pacific coast in Venice, California, which allow for denser urban living in what previously had been a more suburban situation. Abbot Kinney Boulevard is a developing community district of artists, designers, and companies living and working between cafes and restaurants. Planned for live-in and work arrangements, there is one unit per building, each of which shares a common vocabulary of forms, colors, and materials—giving the overall appearance of a development larger than it is. At the same time, the separate identity of each vertically oriented town house is maintained. Garage spaces and double-height work areas are located on the ground floor. Living areas begin on the second level with open kitchens, dining and living/work areas opening onto a small internal terrace. The bedrooms are on the third level, with a private terrace looking out to the street. The designation and use of rooms is purposely vague in order to encourage different options for living and working. A base of exposed concrete block is designed in a pattern to reveal a steel frame structure, within which are placed stucco panels of bright colors. On the street side, the architectural vocabulary recalls R. M. Schindler's work in Los Angeles—an appropriate precedent for these urban villas near the ocean.

KUTH / RANIERI
ARCHITECTS

PARK PRESIDIO TOWN HOUSE
SAN FRANCISCO, CALIFORNIA

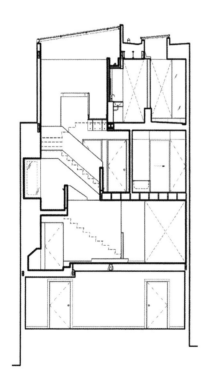

Characterized by numerous vignettes and tableaux of juxtaposed materials and details, this 6,500-square-foot, four-story town house is set in a dense residential area near San Francisco's Park Presidio. The street facade, composed of smooth-troweled plaster punctuated by an aluminum storefront glazing system, is overlayed by a photographic silkscreen image of an aerial view of San Francisco.

The architects have transformed the very narrow front lawn by excavating the width of the lot and dividing the sloped site into a metal entry bridge and a vehicular ramp to the garage. The ground floor is drawn together by a 75-foot-long gallery with terrazzo floors and commercial rubber stair treads for pedestrian traffic. This public space is flanked by the living and dining rooms, family kitchen, main vertical stair core, and rear garden.

Ascending the four levels of the town house by the main stair, illuminated by a skylight above, one experiences sweeping views of the Golden Gate Bridge and the Pacific Ocean beyond the trees of the rear garden. This is made possible by the transparent rear facade, which reads as a glass and aluminum inversion of the vocabulary of the front facade, crowned by an enclosed lookout room and a roof terrace protected by a glass-enclosed handrail.

A self-sufficient energy system is provided by a field of crystalline silicon photovoltaic modules with a 150-square-foot photovoltaic skylight of laminated glass and amorphous cellular technology enclosing the main stair. This is one of the first applications of such a system in the United States. The skylight floods the entire stairwell, illuminating its translucent handrails and the surfaces of adjoining rooms and foyer below.

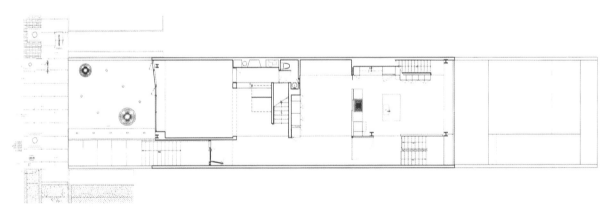

FIRST FLOOR PLAN

GATES MERKULOVA
ARCHITECTS

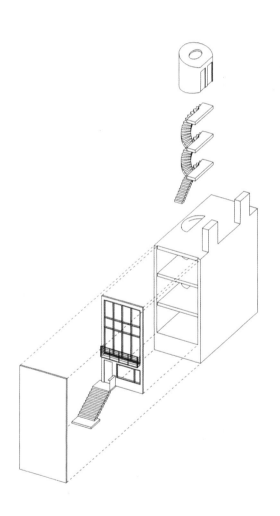

WEIL TOWN HOUSE
NEW YORK, NEW YORK

In this radical transformation of a 1790s Greenwich Village town house, the architects have replaced the deteriorating interior and rear facades with a new structure marked by modern loft-style living and transparency. The home's street facade is of red brick, restored to blend with the surrounding neighborhood and preserve its historic character. Unusual for New York, the main entrance to the house is actually located in the private rear yard, through a courtyard shared with three other townhouses. Here a fountain masks street noise, while a landscape of potted plants and vine-covered brick walls retain a sense of the home's antiquity. Dual entrances also allow the home to be arranged as a two-family residence.

The surprising rear facade is constructed of an aluminum and glass skin that replaced old, structurally unsound masonry. Large sliding doors and a rear balcony allow the outdoor space to penetrate the interior, with maximum ventilation and natural light. Open loft spaces on all three floors continue themes of transparency and light from the exterior of the house. Richly textured and colored translucent planes used in preference to walls make the limited space as open and expansive as possible.

An open-riser steel stair, half-oval in plan, dynamically winds upward toward a small sky-lit interior room at the roof level. The stair doubles as a vertical gallery, where the photographer-owner displays her work upon glass panels inserted into the wall enveloping the stair.

The roof is developed as a private garden, loosely divided into two areas: a secluded, vine-covered pergola at one end, and an open space at the other. Again, a balance is struck between the modern and original elements: the roof terrace's spatial quality is defined by oversized architectural elements: the aluminum-clad stair bulkhead and the masonry fireplace chimney both surrounded by luxuriant vegetation.

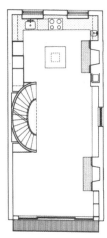

SECOND FLOOR PLAN

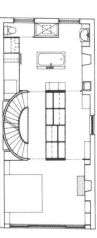

THIRD FLOOR PLAN

JIM JENNINGS
ARCHITECTURE

SOMA TOWN HOUSE
SAN FRANCISCO, CALIFORNIA

Set in San Francisco's South of Market district, where high-end residences mingle with worn-down industrial buildings, this two-story townhouse of weathered Corten steel appears like the hall of a mysterious secret society. The rusting facade is perforated to allow light to penetrate a glass pane fourteen inches behind the metal. The effect is like that of an out of focus film projector, displaying fragmented images of the street on the opposite wall. This creates an almost holographic effect upon the glass shower wall in the master bathroom.

The 4,500-square-foot structure was designed for two former business partners. The main house fronting the street is connected—through an extensive courtyard landscaped with pebbles and bamboo and enclosed by planks of Alaskan yellow cedar—to a smaller structure containing a garage and a guesthouse on the second floor.

The main house divides its space between work and play. A spacious 20-foot-high living/dining room may be used for entertaining, while a kitchen, pantry, and study occupy the other side of the main floor. Poured concrete walls enclose the narrow mahogany stair, recalling the original perimeter walls of the residence's former incarnation as a small industrial building. The stairs lead to the more intimate spaces of two master bedrooms.

Storage space is minimally intrusive, taking the form of concave shelves within the walls, notably above the bed. Narrow rectangular skylights shed sunlight from the gently curved ceilings, accentuating the clean modern lines of the residence and the openness of the space. Translucent partitions hidden in wall recesses can be employed to separate the rooms into four quadrants. The rooms immediately behind the street facade may thus be transformed into an office/conference area.

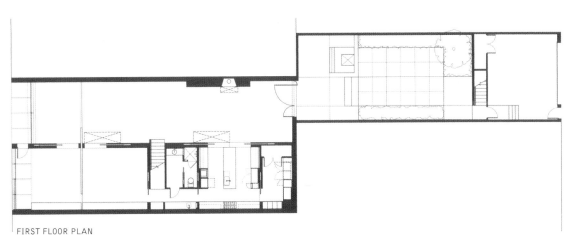

FIRST FLOOR PLAN

JOSEPH VANCE
ARCHITECTS

KRAKOFF TOWN HOUSE
NEW YORK, NEW YORK

Anchored by a triple-height (30-foot-high) living room with a view to the sculpture garden and reflecting pool outside, this town house in Manhattan is home to the owners' eclectic collection of twentieth-century European and American furniture and art. The design intent was to create the kind of timeworn character of a home that had been lived in for generations, starting with a derelict and half-gutted shell.

Minimal detailing and simple geometries result in a combination of modernism and neoclassicism, appropriate to the owners' idiosyncratic collection and entertaining habits. In this spirit, the neoclassical French facade is executed in grooved stucco. Herringbone oak floors add warmth to the public rooms on the lower floors, while an intimate breakfast nook and an extensive library are preferred to a more formal dining space on the first floor.

The library is a fine example of the array of furniture and design objects in the residence. A 1920s Jean Dunand table sits atop an André Arbus carpet from the 1940s, which complements a set of Ruhlmann chairs (another set is found before the window wall in the living room) flanking the bookshelves. A Diego Giacometti wire chair sits opposite the stairwell. The sculptural plaster spiral ascends from the first floor to Delphine's design studio on the third.

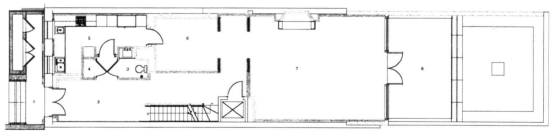

FIRST FLOOR PLAN

STUDIO RINALDI

UPPER WEST SIDE TOWN HOUSE
NEW YORK, NEW YORK

The redesign of this two-story town house creates a new rear facade, an aluminum and glass curtain wall that extends the project to its new focal point, the garden. The rest of the house is designed to extend the openness of this courtyard feature. While original oak details are preserved in the floor, fireplaces, doors, and wainscoting, glass partitions and doors have been installed to divide rooms for privacy and provide natural light and translucency. The dining room is illuminated with new curving glass bay windows and separated from the kitchen by a glass fiber-optic box, which appears as a double-helix of light growing from the floor. Thus natural light is allowed to penetrate as far as the master bathroom and sauna, located in the center of the ground floor and enclosed with translucent glass doors and tile.

The convenience stair accessible from the living room and landing facing the garden is made of sandblasted polycarbonate risers. The oak steps appear to float up from the courtyard to the second story landing and balcony. Sandblasted polycarbonate is similarly used for shelves and vertical elements in the study adjacent to the first floor landing.

The garden itself, conceived by the architect as the final room of the town house is an amalgam of materials and textures. The ground is an irregular checkerboard pattern of polished French limestone and gravestones covered in plexiglass. This contrasts with the rough Brazilian quartzite of the walls and the original red brick of the adjoining house, a reminder of the original structure. This exterior room is furnished with a teakwood bench, steel channels (the same materials used on the first floor balcony), and a vertical concrete fountain and pool.

SECOND FLOOR PLAN

FIRST FLOOR PLAN

STANLEY SAITOWITZ /
NATOMA ARCHITECTS

YERBA BUENA TOWN HOUSES
SAN FRANCISCO, CALIFORNIA

Though this nine-story, vertically oriented town house extends beyond general restrictions for the type, it successfully synthesizes industrial and domestic scales. It appears as a series of town houses along the street, belying its height by an architectural sleight of hand. The site fronts Folsom and Shipley Streets, between Fourth and Fifth Streets. The project has 190 units of live/work and loft-style spaces; parking and commercial areas are on the ground floor.

Embedded in the lower section of the building are four floors for parking, flanked on both Folsom and Shipley Streets by live/work units. A residential tower, set back on the narrow Shipley side, with two-story loft apartments, forms an urban wall along Folsom. Translucent glass, cube-shaped bay-style windows alternate with carved out balconies, creating an image that is like an extended town house, four stories higher than the general type. The scale is made more intimate by a single exterior frame that encompasses the double-height spaces. The glass cubes project above the roof, creating a crenellated geometric skyline. Exposed, post-tension concrete serves as the interior and exterior finish. At night the translucent and transparent glass bays, framed by the concrete grid, are glowing lanterns for Folsom Street.

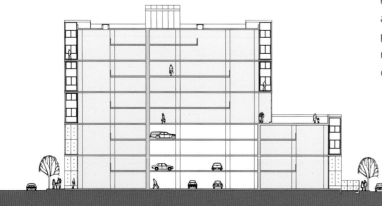

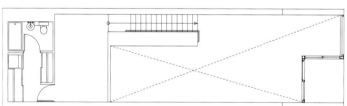

TYPICAL UNIT MEZZANINE FLOOR PLAN

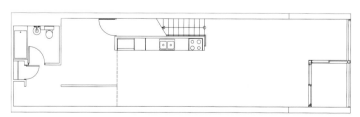

TYPICAL UNIT MAIN LEVEL FLOOR PLAN

GLUCKMAN MAYNER
ARCHITECTS

MERRIN TOWN HOUSE
NEW YORK, NEW YORK

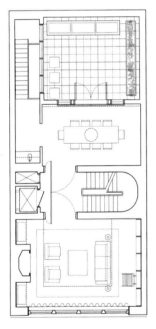

SECOND FLOOR PLAN

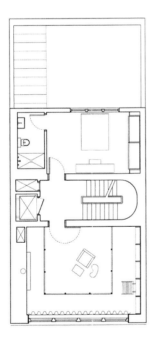

THIRD FLOOR PLAN

Set within a newly constructed town house in the Tribeca section of Lower Manhattan, the concept of a room within a room animates the design. Suspended in the double-height living room, a stainless steel mesh box acts as a small reading room while it creates a more intimate scale on the main level. From the street, this appears as a volume floating within a volume. The room is otherwise defined by pivoting perforated copper door partitions and furnished with heartwood pine bookshelves and copper plate display cabinets.

On the lower level, two large, translucent plastic sliding doors can be moved to alter the size of the media room, where custom aluminum laminate cabinetry houses a large home theater. Custom furniture and cabinet units housing a plasma television were designed for the master bedroom suite. The penthouse office, children's bedrooms and playroom were each outfitted with a custom built-in cantilevered desk and shelf units. Visually unifying the 6-story residence, a vertical aluminum light fixture runs the entire height of the stairwell.

The town house makes use of an innovative mechanical system, a ground source geo-thermal heat pump that extracts its heating and cooling needs from a 1200-foot-deep well below the building, allowing for very low heating and cooling costs. All interior finishes were screened for compliance for "green" architecture, with low emissions of harmful gases.

SMITH THOMPSON
ARCHITECTS

CHELSEA GALLERY AND TOWN HOUSE
NEW YORK, NEW YORK

This extraordinary town house is a series of cubes within cubes, a Russian doll-like composition that anchors the corner with sheets of steel cut open for views of the garden and living areas within. The steel recalls the neighboring High Line, an abandoned elevated train trestle that is currently being renovated as a public park. An art gallery is set on the lower level while above the architects live and work in rooms that open to an internal garden and fragmented views of the urban landscape. The steel envelope provides remarkable sound insulation so that the noisy location is transformed into an oasis of peace and quiet on the interior. These rooms are filled with light and allow lively spatial flow from one space to another. The vocabulary of steel and glass is extended from without to within in elegant details that highlight each space with a sculptural presence that recalls the work of David Smith and, of course, Mies van der Rohe.

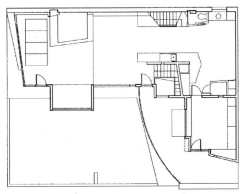

THIRD FLOOR PLAN

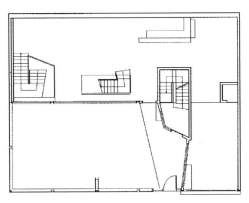

FIRST FLOOR PLAN

LORCAN O'HERLIHY
ARCHITECTS

VERTICAL TOWN HOUSE
LOS ANGELES, CALIFORNIA

This striking town house set between more mundane houses in Venice Beach is prominent for its vertical, asymmetrical pattern of windows on all sides. Sited back from the street and supported on red columns, the house is typically urban, in that its sidewalls are set parallel to those of its neighbors, yet also a modernist object in space, in its contrasting color and the wrap-around, jagged wallpaper effect. The unusual window arrangement is a result planned to mitigate the fact of a narrow lot with views that are not particularly desirable. Its 105 vertical window slits—some clear, some translucent in yellow and blue, and some opaque—provide a gentle cocoon of light that envelops the interior. A welded steel structural frame allows for the window openings in this irregular pattern, something that would be impossible with traditional wood framing techniques. The windows frame certain views and block others out. For maximum light, the kitchen, living, and dining rooms are on the top floor, the two bed rooms and baths are on the second, and a studio for the architect is on the lower level. Built-in furniture in two-tone wood continues the architectural vocabulary of the exterior on the inside. For the architect's wife, who is an actress, a quiet place to study scripts has been positioned atop the roof, and provides views of the Pacific and the Santa Monica Mountains. A red spiral stair affords direct access from the roof terrace to the backyard.

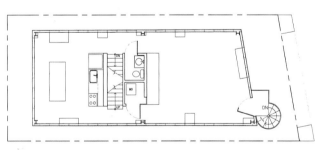

THIRD FLOOR PLAN

SECOND FLOOR PLAN

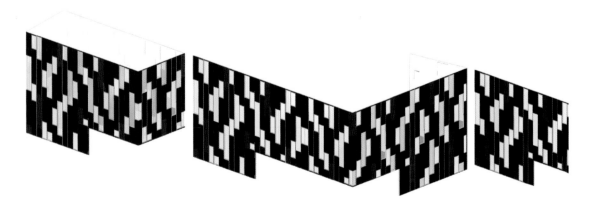

DEAN NOTA
ARCHITECT

REYNA TOWN HOUSE
HERMOSA BEACH, CALIFORNIA

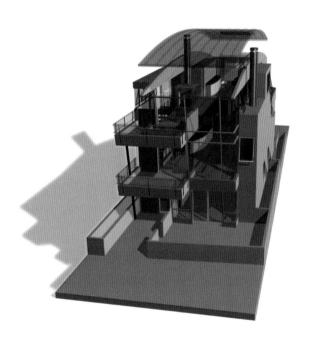

This concrete and glass town house is located on a 30-by-80-foot oceanfront lot at the western edge of metropolitan Los Angeles. The lot is framed by the Hermosa Beach Pier to the north and the Palos Verdes Peninsula to the south. While strikingly convex in form, its upper stories protruding gently outward toward the sea and the street, the residence blends well with older, less remarkable surrounding structures, with which it shares the block.

The color-drenched living spaces on the main floor provide room for entertaining and interaction with the beachfront and the street, with the automobile entrance on the street front and the pedestrian entrance from a walkway adjoining the beach. The levels are joined by a red steel stair core, which leads from the more public space of the ground floor to more private spaces—a dining room, kitchen, and bedroom on the street side—with views to the ocean.

These spaces culminate in a master suite at the top of the stair. This longitudinal vault is a visual axis leading to the rear master bathroom. A red steel bridge extends from the street through the double-height room to a cantilevered observation platform that penetrates the rear window wall, mirrored by a similar deck on the first floor. While privacy increases on the upper floors, the permeation of natural light and views to the ocean and horizon become increasingly dramatic.

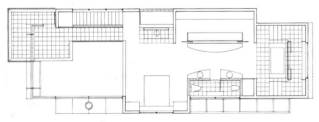

SECOND FLOOR PLAN

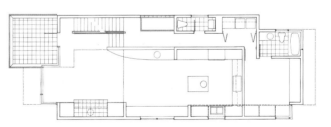

THIRD FLOOR PLAN

JOHN PETRARCA
ARCHITECT

READE STREET TOWN HOUSE
NEW YORK, NEW YORK

The black-painted recycled steel facade of this 6,000-square-foot town house a few blocks from the World Trade Center Site echoes the cast-iron architecture of the surrounding neighborhood in a distinctly modern manner. The house has become a neighborhood landmark in the formerly industrial Tribeca area. Before Mr. Petrarca's untimely death in 2003, the structure was the architect-owner's office and home, housing his five-person architecture firm on the main floor.

The townhouse's grandness belies its imaginative approach to green architecture. The architect and his wife selected French limestone (from Amarlo) and oiled wood floors, natural wood finishes, and low-toxic paints, designing all of the furniture themselves. The main living/dining space is located on the fourth floor, with a 20-foot-high ceiling and a fireplace ensconced in black Chinese quartzite and walnut paneling. Marmoleum, a natural linoleum, was applied to kitchen cabinetry in collaboration with Bulthaup. The dramatic stairwell is constructed of recycled glass slabs and inexpensive industrial stainless steel mesh.

A completely geothermal heating system makes this home the first of its kind in New York City. A system of pipes extend 1,200 feet (the height of the Empire State Building) into the earth, where the temperature remains constant at fifty-two degrees. To trap heat, the home is built of insulated concrete structural forms (ICFs)—made of styrofoam joined to concrete—which also leave no space for insects to nest. At sixty-two feet, the building is the tallest ever constructed with these materials.

The building receives a tremendous amount of sunlight during the day. More importantly, the special structural and ventilation systems minimized environmental dust and debris in the wake of the WTC tragedy.

FOURTH FLOOR PLAN

THIRD FLOOR PLAN

BRINNINSTOOL
+ LYNCH, LTD.

OLD TOWN TOWN HOUSE
CHICAGO, ILLINOIS

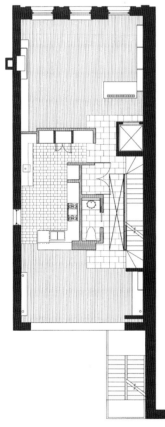

FIRST FLOOR PLAN

Contrasting old and new, this three-story nineteenth-century town house was renovated for retail space on street level and as a residence on the top two floors. In the rear of the lot, a courtyard was reconstructed as a place of refuge and the focus of views from the house. A coach house in this courtyard was rebuilt as a garage and a guesthouse with a kitchen to allow for entertaining and dining in good weather. The street facade was restored within historic guidelines, while the interior was opened to maximize natural light and air, in an elegant, spare, minimal style. A stairway of steel, slate, wood, and glass begins in the lower hallway and culminates under the skylight of the third floor. As a convenience allowing items to be carried easily from the basement to the upper floors, an elevator was installed adjacent to the stairway. Wood floors were used in the main rooms, with slate for the hallways and bathrooms, and cork for the kitchen. Millwork volumes, held away from the ceilings, define the living spaces and function as cabinetry and shelving. All detailing emphasizes the separation and distinction between materials, heightening their unique character and richness. Spatially, the light of the courtyard flows through the house, so that its tranquil setting permeates the experience of living close to nature in the midst of the urban environment.

STANLEY SAITOWITZ /
NATOMA ARCHITECTS

1110 GREEN STREET TOWN HOUSE
SAN FRANCISCO, CALIFORNIA

This simple but dramatic townhouse renovation in the Russian Hill neighborhood is remarkable for its stunning facade, reclad in charcoal-painted cement, extending to a cement-clad front entry door and garage door. Channels in the glass window-cubes cut into the facade seem to intersect the horizontal lines of the cement planks.

Consistency was paramount for the architect in his selection of materials, which find their parallel on the interior in the form of slate floors, polished slate stairs (as well as sink and whirlpool tub casing) and thick etched glass walls, handrails, and Antonio Citterio tables. These materials are also canine-friendly, a plus for the owner who is a breeder of championship Pekinese.

A new skylight illuminates the glass, selected by the architect to pick up the bay's changing greens. The angled stairwell becomes the shining core of the house, with abstracted geometric forms flickering in and out of the eye as one ascends toward the light. Views of the bay and the city can also be taken in from a living room terrace on the fifth floor, a chef's kitchen on the fourth, and a soundproof media room on the third floor.

While unique for its bold monumentality and fortress-like facade, the true genius of this design is its subtle appreciation and integration with the surrounding urban land and seascapes from which it rises.

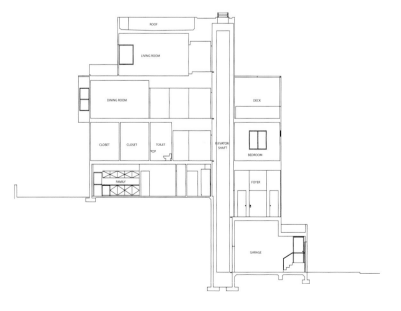

THIRD FLOOR PLAN

FOURTH FLOOR PLAN

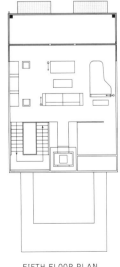

FIFTH FLOOR PLAN

LESLIE GILL
ARCHITECT

WEST SIDE TOWN HOUSE
NEW YORK, NEW YORK

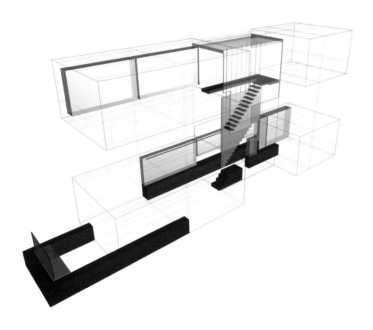

The challenge in this row house on a street on the Upper West Side of Manhattan was to create a "country home," a place of repose in the midst of chaotic city living. The 1600-square-foot space had unusual spatial constraints, even by the abnormally severe standards of New York City. The typical brownstone affords a width of 20 to 25 feet, while this site alllowed only 16 feet at its widest and 9 feet at its most compressed. The task was to take this narrow dark space and create an open light-filled place that incorporates nature within the metropolitan context. This was miraculously achieved by the use of an hourglass plan, which has the house wider at each end and compressed in the middle. To amplify the light, vertical surfaces were sheathed in a highly reflective plaster. At the core, artificial light was introduced and made to cascade down the two-story opening of the stair well. The exquisitely detailed staircase with floating treads bounded by a metal screen was designed to create spatial differentiation while allowing visual permeability. A bridge at the upper level connects the two bedrooms, allowing more light to flow down the atrium-like feature of the stair. A luxuriantly planted roof terrace off the dining room and a custom designed aquarium bring the concept of the miniature landscape into the house.

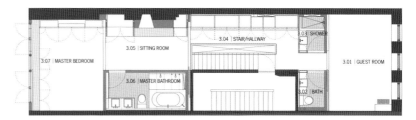

THIRD FLOOR PLAN

| 3.07 | MASTER BEDROOM | 3.05 | SITTING ROOM | 3.04 | STAIR/HALLWAY | 3.03 | SHOWER | 3.01 | GUEST ROOM |
| 3.06 | MASTER BATHROOM | 3.02 | BATH |

SECOND FLOOR PLAN

JONATHAN SEGAL
ARCHITECT

TITAN TOWN HOUSES
LA JOLLA, CALIFORNIA

Directly adjacent to the San Diego Freeway, this urban housing development boasts 22 lofts with two story living spaces, on-grade parking and a courtyard that provides a safe environment and encourages neighbor interaction in a challenging neighborhood. On the street facade, long narrow window walls open to balconies and illuminate the living/dining/kitchen areas on the main floor. At night the buildings become glowing cubes of light, their alternating concrete and copper-toned steel facades generating a bright and welcoming presence on the street.

The interior takes advantage of this characteristic with double-height space in the front of the house receding to dining and food preparation areas beneath the second floor lofts. An angular plaster stair rail joins the handrail of the upper floor's window-lined walkway/bridge that leads back to the master bedroom and baths on the upper stories.

Simplicity and density of plan are the result of a tight budget. By eliminating the elevator and interior corridors, the architect added the space and cost savings to the individual units, envisioning a new prototype for four-story rental unit housing. Each apartment has oversized glazing, soaring ceilings and wood floors on the main level.

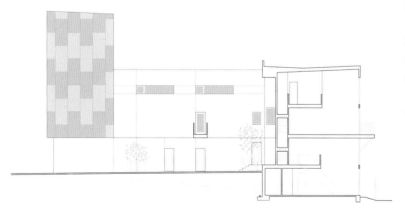

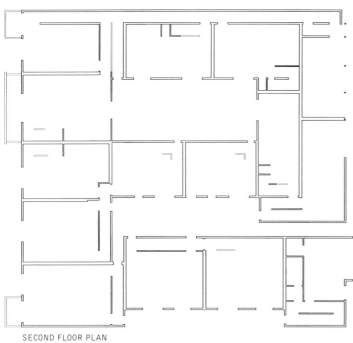

SECOND FLOOR PLAN

ALEXANDER GORLIN
ARCHITECTS

CHICAGO TOWN HOUSE
CHICAGO, ILLINOIS

FIRST FLOOR PLAN

This town house for a bachelor in the Bucktown section of Chicago is a gleaming modern structure that floats above its more traditional neighbors. Set back behind a brick-walled garden, a steel and stone stair cuts through the volume of the house leading directly from the street to the main living level on the second floor and beyond to the third level and roof terraces above. On the main level, a double-height space contains the open loft of the kitchen, living, and dining areas. The vertically oriented living room is framed by large expanses of glass, which open onto the garden below and provide views of the street. Above, the suspended glass box of the master bedroom and bathroom floats. The sensual space of the glass shower and freestanding tub is directly open to the master bedroom blurring the boundaries between these traditionally separate areas. At both ends, glass walls afford views of the city. The clothes closet is completely open to view, where the client's perfectly coordinated suits hang for all the world to see, allowing him to "shop" daily for his suit of choice—recalling perhaps a scene for American Gigolo. Above is a terrace with views to downtown Chicago. A luminous screen of parachute cloth curtains—a theatrical gesture—defines the space of the dining room, with its own terrace above the garage. On the lower level are a guest bedroom and an exercise space. Materials are limited to a minimally cool palette of white painted steel, white statuary marble for all counters, gray-toned stone floors from China, and white plaster walls.

SECOND FLOOR PLAN

McINTURFF
ARCHITECTS

GEORGETOWN TOWN HOUSE
WASHINGTON, D.C.

This home in the Georgetown area affords some of the most dramatic views available in Washington, DC, overlooking the city as well as the Potomac River. This project, which began as a minor renovation of bathrooms, brought about the discovery of a much more serious structural failure. A four-story rear addition was in fact splitting away from the main body of the house. This portion of the home, dating from the 1970s, had been migrating south as the result of its construction upon sixty feet of fill.

This is neatly remedied by the architects' insertion of helical piers and a new frame, all of black steel, and integrated with an exterior stair. The window-wall in the rear is protected from the sun by teakwood mullions and shades. These elements parallel an interior stair core of the same materials, which one traverses through elegantly layered frosted plexiglass, wood, and steel.

Removal of a floor creates a double-height space in the rear from which to appreciate views of the garden and the city. Portions of the original brick exterior surround the new window wall and join brick walls surrounding the garden.

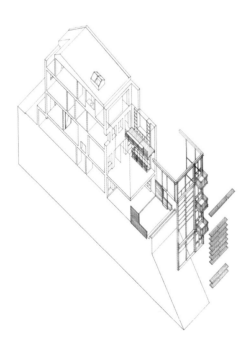

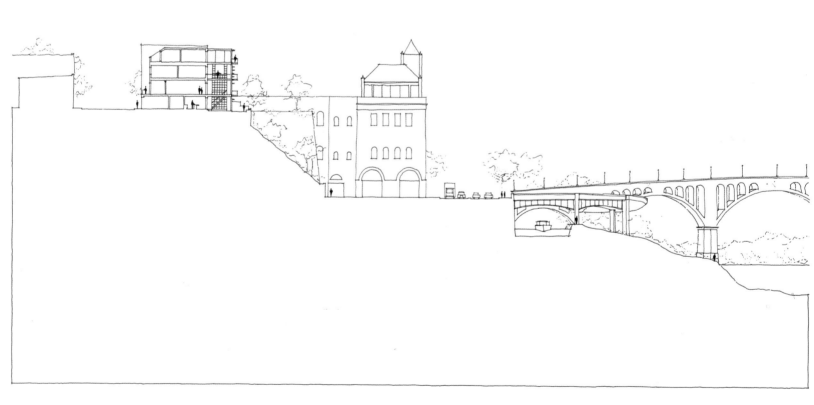

MICHAEL STRAUSS &
DOROTHY HOM

PRIVATE TOWN HOUSE
NEW YORK, NEW YORK

THIRD FLOOR PLAN

This former commercial structure in the West Village was transformed into a stunning 8,000-square-foot, five-story mixed-use building with residential space on the four upper levels. Ground-floor commercial space is divided into three bays. The eye-catching stucco facade with anodized steel reveals projects a rectangular box of bay windows on the third and fourth stories. The home's main living space lies behind, a twenty-foot cube that takes advantage of views down West 13th Street and to lower Manhattan via West 4th Street.

Details include an orange glass window near the ceiling and a small niche in the wall (formerly a fireplace) designed to reflect candlelight. Furniture selected by the architects reflects the clients' interest in antique-Asian and modern-Italian design. An array of unusual finishes include ribbon mahogany and white-washed oak. The intimate dining room is ensconced in cerused English chestnut with oiled, cold-rolled steel picture rails. All cabinetry is custom-designed.

Owners enter through a private elevator and an intimate foyer with a dramatic orange wall finished in textured faux shagreen. A cantilevered custom steel and fluted glass stair core leads also to the living room and through the fourth floor mezzanine library, child, and guest bedrooms. It terminates at the fifth-story master bedroom, master bath, and walk-in closet. The third, fourth, and fifth floors are extended to create a dramatic series of stepped terraces, the fifth story terrace housing a large rose garden.

ZACK / DE VITO
ARCHITECTURE

STATES STREET TOWN HOUSE
SAN FRANCISCO, CALIFORNIA

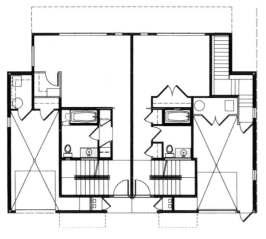

FIRST FLOOR PLAN

This home in the Castro District of San Francisco perches on a sloped hillside overlooking the city. The street facade is of custom-finished concrete and steel, and projects bronzed steel-encased window boxes toward the street. The third floor is a vaulted space encircled by large clerestory windows. The arched roof curves downward from the street to the rear of the house, breaks into steel awnings, and finally into glass panes, providing both sunlight and shade to rear terraces with views into the city.

The third floor terraces sit atop the second floor, whose volume projects farther down the hillside, again in the form of bronzed steel-wrapped bay windows. The ground floor is also terraced, extending farther down the hill horizontally, and is accessible by the main stair core of the house. These terraces extend to the south and east, offering views corresponding to the hill's slopes in both directions.

The stark white interior of the town house is provided maximum light by large clerestory windows. The arched metal roofs also provide loft-like spaces within. Floors of custom-finished concrete are complemented by extensive use of steel and glass furnishings, notably the third-story fireplace of weathered steel, its exposed chimney-vent projecting a vertical steel element centering the open dining/kitchen space that houses it.

Exposed white steel trusses with attached track lighting give the space a transparent ultramodern feel, while the translucent glass handrail of the stair core helps disperse the light throughout the house.

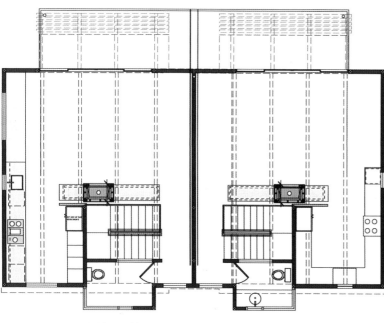

SECOND FLOOR PLAN

BROMLEY CALDARI
ARCHITECTS

EAST 55TH STREET TOWN HOUSES
NEW YORK, NEW YORK

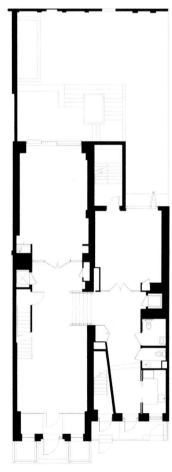

FIRST FLOOR PLAN

Two adjoining town houses were combined into one live/work organization through the introduction of a stair that reconciles the different floor heights of each house. This space also acts as an atrium, allowing a skylight to flood the interior with natural light at its most distant point from the windows at each end. The town houses are used for a business development company and as the residence of one of the owners, who occupies the top two floors of the five-story house. The rooftop duplex has a double-height space dominated by a very large walnut cabinet featuring a distinguished collection of African masks. An open walnut stair leads up to the rebuilt sunroom and the bridge to the bedrooms. The fifth floor master bedroom is set back to form a terrace on the roof of the fourth floor. Since the owner is an avid wood aficionado, the architects obliged by specifying numerous exotic woods, such as wenge, sapelle, and tamo, which in addition to walnut, give a darkly luxurious feeling to the house.

FOURTH FLOOR PLAN

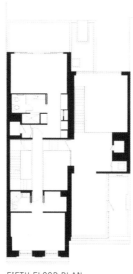

FIFTH FLOOR PLAN

TANNERHECHT
ARCHITECTURE

CANNERY TOWN HOUSES
NEWPORT BEACH, CALIFORNIA

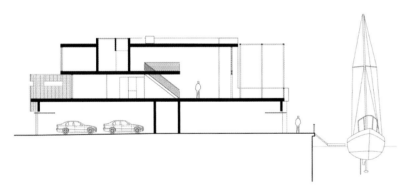

Comprised of twenty-two mixed-use town houses in Newport Beach, these units employ the California coastline's best assets: light, air, and water. The ground floor of each building is designed for commercial use, as required by the planning guidelines of Cannery Village. Two upper floors provide residential space, allowing for a work-at-home lifestyle option for small-scale professional service businessmen and encouraging an interactive, pedestrian-oriented streetscape. Parking, as well as landscaped residential space, is located in breezeways: long linear bands between lots, which minimize the number of parked cars on the street frontage.

Clean and elegant modern interiors are achieved with the use of brushed steel structural elements and handrails, set against clean white wooden and cinder block walls. Industrial materials, such as fluted metal siding, guardrails, and exposed mechanical equipment on rooftops, contribute to the design's unique identity. The design is clearly inspired by historic residences, local forms and materials, and marine buildings throughout the historic Cannery Village district.

Other interior features include exposed steel and wood structural elements and large skylights. Light is diffused throughout each unit through the use of retracting window walls, operable clerestory windows, while deep overhangs blur the line between interior and exterior. Even cabinetry is designed with translucent materials to allow light to penetrate kitchens.

The top story of each building's waterfront facade is composed of a double-height window wall opening onto a terrace lightly enclosed by a steel lattice. The result is a stunning view to the harbor and the projection of a clear architectural identity in harmony with light industrial surroundings.

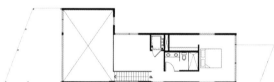

THIRD FLOOR PLAN

SECOND FLOOR PLAN

FIRST FLOOR PLAN

HARIRI AND HARIRI
ARCHITECTURE

PERRY STREET TOWN HOUSE
NEW YORK, NEW YORK

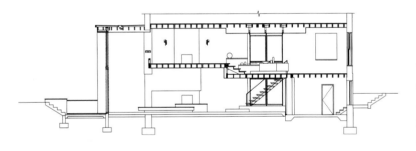

This apparently typical brownstone town house for a product designer, located in Greenwich Village, houses an impressive collection of art and artifacts. While there is no gallery space per se, the house represents the intersection of art and architecture and serves as a giant backdrop for his pieces. Entering the space on the upper level, a double-height light wall greets visitors, sheds light on the art, and connects the home vertically and organizing circulation. The lofted first floor is defined by a steel railing containing a series of embedded candles. The entry hall is separated from the adjoining library/bedroom by a screen designed by the owner. Kitchen, shower, and powder room along the east wall are located behind translucent screens on tracks that glow and expose the adjacent spaces when opened. The bathroom sink is a trough of rough-hewn stone that sits upon the steel countertop, complemented by a stone carving displayed beside it.

Along the light wall, a metal stair with frosted translucent treads lead downstairs to the living room. Two polished concrete slabs transition into the main living room, designed entirely of this material and again generously complemented by pieces from the owner's collection. These are beautifully displayed on the low mantle of the sculptural stucco fireplace, also joined to the room with a concrete wall and stepped concrete floor. The rear of the living room adjoins the terrace and garden space through large sliding glass doors. A pool of water carved into the floor at the edge of the room continues outside through a water channel beneath the doors. The water flows from a fountain composed of a piece of carved Indian marble from the Mogul period.

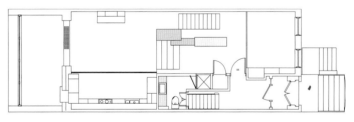

SECOND FLOOR PLAN

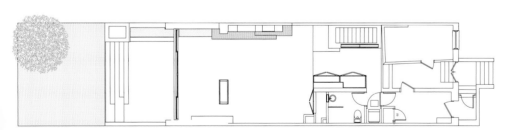

FIRST FLOOR PLAN

PROJECT CREDITS

1100 ARCHITECTS
VILLAGE RESIDENCE
Project Principal: David Piscuskas
Structural Engineer: Robert Silman Associates, PC
Mechanical Engineer: D'Antonio Consulting Engineers
Lighting: Johnson Schwinghammer

BRININSTOOL + LYNCH, LTD.
OLD TOWN TOWN HOUSE
Project Principal: Bradley Lynch
Structural Engineer: Lyle Haag Engineering

BROMLEY CALDARI ARCHITECTS
EAST 55TH STREET TOWN HOUSES
Project Principals: Jerry Caldari, Scott Bromley
Structural Engineer: LZA Technology
Mechanical Engineer: GC Eng Associates

GATES MERKULOVA ARCHITECTS
WEIL TOWN HOUSE
Project Principals: Paul Gates, Zhenya Merkulova
Structural Engineer: John D. Nakrosis Building Design
Mechanical Engineer: Athwal Associates
Landscape Architect: Thomas Navin

LESLIE GILL ARCHITECT
WEST SIDE TOWN HOUSE
Project Principal: Leslie Gill
Structural Engineer: Rodney D. Gibble Consulting Engineers
Mechanical Engineer: Andrew Collins PE

GLUCKMAN MAYNER ARCHITECTS
MERRIN TOWN HOUSE
Project Principal: Richard Gluckman, FAIA
Interior Designer: Nina Seirafi
Mechanical Engineer: M.A. Rubiano, P.C.
Landscape Architect: Evan Lai Landscape, New York, NY
Building Architect: Studio Petrarca

ALEXANDER GORLIN ARCHITECTS
NEW YORK TOWN HOUSE
Project Principal: Alexander Gorlin
Structural Engineer: Ross Dalland
Interior Designers: EFM Design, Stephen Sclaroff
Lighting: Kugler Tillotson Associates
Landscape Architects: Matthews/Nielsen

ALEXANDER GORLIN ARCHITECTS
CHICAGO TOWN HOUSE
Project Principal: Alexander Gorlin
Structural Engineer: Frank A. Gusinde Jr., The Structural Shop
Mechanical Engineer: Sheldon Lazan, PE
Architect of Record: Ed Kuypers

ROBERT M. GURNEY, AIA
CALVERT STREET TOWN HOUSE
Project Principal: Robert M. Gurney, AIA
Interior Design: Therese Baron Gurney, ASID

HARIRI AND HARIRI ARCHITECTURE
PERRY STREET TOWN HOUSE
Project Principals: Gisue Hariri, Mojgan Hariri
Structural Engineer: Robert Silman Associates, PC
Mechanical Engineer: Szekely Engineering

CHRISTIAN HUBERT STUDIO
DAVID SALLE TOWN HOUSE
Design Architect: Christian Hubert
Associate Architect: David Fratianne
Structural Engineer: Robert Silman Associates, PC
Mechanical Engineer: Vogel Taylor
Landscape Architects: R/F Associates

JIM JENNINGS ARCHITECTURE
SOMA TOWN HOUSE
Project Principal: Jim Jennings
Structural Engineer: Santos & Urrutia
Lighting: Dan Dodt, John Wigmore (light sculptures)

JOSEPH VANCE ARCHITECTS
KRAKOFF TOWN HOUSE
Project Principals: Reed and Delphine Krakoff, Pamplemousse Design;
Joseph Vance Architects (project architect)

KUTH/RANIERI ARCHITECTS
PARK PRESIDIO TOWN HOUSE
Project Principals: Byron Kuth, Liz Ranieri
Structural Engineer: Lang Engineering
Photovoltaic: High Sun Engineering
Lighting: Architecture and Light

MACK ARCHITECTS
ABBOT KINNEY TOWN HOUSES, BAY CITIES TOWN HOUSES
Project Principal: Mark Mack

MARPILLERO POLLAK ARCHITECTS
DUANE STREET TOWN HOUSE
Project Principals: Sandro Marpillero, AIA, Partner-in-Charge;
Linda Pollak, AIA

MCINTURFF ARCHITECTS
GEORGETOWN TOWN HOUSE
Project Principal: Mark McInturff

DEAN NOTA ARCHITECT
REYNA RESIDENCE
Project Principal: Dean A. Nota, AIA
Structural Engineer: Orland Engineering
Interiors: Marina Mirzuh, Chimera Interiors

LORCAN O'HERLIHY ARCHITECTS
VERTICAL TOWN HOUSE
Project Principal: Lorcan O'Herlihy
Structural Engineer: Paul Franceschi

JOHN PETRARCA ARCHITECT
READE STREET TOWN HOUSE
Project Principal: John L. Petrarca
Structural Engineer: Hage Engineering
Mechanical Engineer: Andrew Collins, PE
Geothermal Consultant: Carl Orio, Water & Energy Systems Corp.

STUDIO RINALDI
UPPER WEST SIDE TOWN HOUSE
Project Principal: Stefania Rinaldi
Engineer/Architect of Record: Elie Geiger, PE, Geiger Engineering, PC
Landscape Designer: Story, Paula Hayes principal

STANLEY SAITOWITZ/NATOMA ARCHITECTS INC.
YERBA BUENA TOWN HOUSES
Project Principal: Stanley Saitowitz
Structural Engineer: Watry Design Group
Mechanical Engineer: ACCO

STANLEY SAITOWITZ/NATOMA ARCHITECTS INC.
1110 GREEN STREET TOWN HOUSE
Project Principal: Stanley Saitowitz

JONATHAN SEGAL ARCHITECT
TITAN TOWN HOUSES
Project Principal: Jonathan Segal, FAIA

SHELTON, MINDEL & ASSOCIATES
HISTORIC TOWN HOUSE
Project Principals: Lee F. Mindel, Peter Shelton

SMITH & THOMPSON ARCHITECTS
CHELSEA GALLERY AND TOWN HOUSE
Project Principals: G. Phillip Smith, Douglas Thompson
Structural Engineer: Rand Engineering

MICHAEL STRAUSS AND DOROTHY HOM
WEST VILLAGE TOWN HOUSE
Project Principals and Builders: Michael J. Strauss,
Dorothy Hom, Vanguard Construction and Development Co., Inc.
Project Architect: Byrns Kendall Schifferdecker
Structural Engineer: Avishay I. Mazor P.E.
Mechanical Engineer: Martin Haber Engineers
Lighting: Ann Schiffers

TANNERHECHT ARCHITECTURE
CANNERY TOWN HOUSES
Project Principals: David Hecht, Jim Tanner
Structural Engineer: Van Dorpe Chou Associates
Mechanical Engineer: KMA Engineers
Landscape Architect: MJS Design Group

VALERIO DEWALT TRAIN ASSOCIATES
DOBLIN TOWN HOUSE
Project Principal: Joe Valerio
Structural Engineer: Robert Darvas Associates
Lighting: Charter Sills + Associates

WESLEY WEI ARCHITECTS
TOWN HOUSE WITH SIX WALLS
Project Principal: Wesley Wei FAIA
Lighting: OLC – Philadelphia
Art Installation: Louise Strawbridge + Diane Messinger

ZACK / DE VITO ARCHITECTURE
STATES STREET TOWN HOUSE
Project Principals: Jim Zack and Lise de Vito
Structural Engineer: Santos and Urrutia

CREDITS

Introduction: p. 6 Brian Rose; p. 8 top Editions Sand (Androuet du Cerceau, Les Plus Excellents Bastiments de France; 1560, reprint by David Thompson, Paris, 1988), p. 8 bottom Library of Congress, Prints and Photographs Division, Reproduction Number LC-USZ62-24784; p. 9 left Het Utrechts Archief (Municipal Archive of Utrecht, Holland), p. 9 right Jordi Bernardo, reproduced from HILBERSEIMER / MIES VAN DER ROHE: Lafayette Park Detroit, ed. Charles Waldheim (Cambridge, Mass. and Munich: Harvard Graduate School of Design and Prestel, 2004); p.10 top Library of Congress, Prints & Photographs Division, Gottscho-Schleisner Collection, Reproduction Number LC-G612-T01-58303, p.10 bottom Peter Aaron/ESTO; p. 11 Paul Warchol; p.12 Ezra Stoller/ESTO; p. 13 top Paul Kolnik p.13 bottom Michael Moran; p.14 2001 Aqua; p.15 Peter Aaron/ESTO.

Peter Aaron, ESTO: pp. 61-65, 75-85
Massimiliano Bolzonella: pp. 217-219
dna_la: pp.159, 160 (right)
Brendan Dunnigan: pp. 227-228
Elizabeth Felicella: pp. 19-27
Jimmy Fluker/Colony: 191-193
Leslie Gill: pp. 185-189
Justin Goldberg/ESTO: pp. 53-59

J.B. Grant: pp. 101-105
Tim Griffith: 131-137, 177-183
Hariri and Hariri Architecture: p.236 (left)
David Hecht: p. 229
Julia Heine / McInturff Architects: pp. 205-209
Anice Hoachlander: pp.29, 30 (left), 34
Barbara Karant: pp. 67-73
Eric Laignel: pp. 221-225
Michael Moran: pp. 45-51,195-203
Photography Erhard Pfeiffer: pp.160 (left), 161-163
Toby Ponnay: pp.230-231
Undine Pröhl: pp. 87-93, 156-157
Sharon Risedorph: pp. 95, 96 (left),107-113
Cesar Rubio: pp. 96 (right), 97-99
Matthias Petrus Schaller: pp. 115-123
Catherine Tighe Photographer: pp. 37-43
Paul Warchol: pp. 30 (right), 31-33, 35, 165-169, 211-215, 233-235, 236 (right), 237
Michael Weschler: pp. 153-155
Harry Zernike: pp. 139-143
Wade Zimmerman: pp. 125-129

ACKNOWLEDGMENTS

I am grateful to the legendary David Morton for his guidance and inspiration. To Dung Ngo for his beautiful and crisp design. Douglas Curran was a meticulous editor. Richard Hayes contributed greatly with his research and scholarship. And to Leo Jilk, for his organizational talents.